Beverly Bedeviled:
One Town's True Connections
with the Witchcraft of 1692

"At a meeting of the Selectmen February ye 170 4/3
Received with Jonathan Rayment for Timber for a pare
of Stairs & for halling ye Timber to our meeting
house."—Vol. ii. page 124. B.T.R.

"Ordered that Collector Robert Morgan pay
unto Peter Greves thirteen Shillings & Sixpence
out of the Towns Money in his hands it being
Making & Setting up a Whipping Post.
Robert Hale. Town Cle.
Vol. III p. 555. BT

"Yᵉ OLD MEETING HOUSE, 1682."

"Meeting of the Selectmen 1705 — Paid to Nathaniell Hayward for a Whele for our bel and other work done to meeting house 1.00.00
Paid to Peter Wooding for puting up yᵉ vane of yᵉ meeting house 00.10.00"—Vol. ii p.—

Beverly Bedeviled:
One Town's True Connections
with the Witchcraft of 1692

Edward R. Brown

Beverly Historical Society
Beverly, Massachusetts

First Printing: 2015

ISBN 978-1-891906-10-7

Beverly Historical Society
117 Cabot Street
Beverly, MA 01915

www.beverlyhistory.org

Ordering Information: Special discounts are available on quantity purchases by corporations, associations, educators, and others. For details, contact the publisher at the above listed address.

U.S. trade bookstores and wholesalers: Please contact Beverly Historical Society, 978-922-1186; or email info@beverlyhistory.org

Contents

Foreword

The Strange, Sad Year of 1692

Every year, hundreds of thousands of visitors flock to Salem, Massachusetts. Most are attracted not by the city's illustrious history as a seaport and center of trade, but by the more modern attempts to capitalize financially on the infamous witchcraft trials of 1692. Those events led to the executions of 20 innocent persons (two others died while incarcerated) and disrupted the lives of hundreds of other Essex County residents. Numerous myths have crept in over the years regarding the "witchcraft." Many visitors want to see the place where the witches were "burned," and modern writers, who should know better, have spread the lie of Salem as a center of "witch burning." While such horrifying executions did take place in continental Europe, no "witch" was ever burned to death in Massachusetts. Nineteen of the convicted souls in 1692 died by hanging (which then meant strangulation at the end of a rope), while the 20th died slowly, pressed to death under heavy weights, when he steadfastly refused to enter a plea before the court.

While Salem has usurped credit as the tourist-fueled capital of witchcraft, that connection mainly centers on being the place where the executions took place. The furor of 1692 erupted in Danvers (then called Salem Village), and would spread to a number of other towns. Modern Beverly, for the most part, has stayed out of it, with the exception of a generally discredited claim that an accusation of witchcraft against the wife of the town's minister was what put a stop to the delusion. But Beverly does have its real witchcraft connections, and the most important of those revolve around two 17th century houses owned and maintained by the Beverly Historical Society and Museum – Balch House and Hale House. Those stories go far beyond the realm of myth, and modern-day visitors can see those places and hear the tales told. This little book is an attempt to put Beverly's stories together without myth or lurid sensationalism. After all, real people were involved, not caricatures, although some of them were hardly model citizens.

Many people have the impression that the events of 1692 were unique to Salem. There had been prosecutions for witchcraft earlier in New England, although it must be acknowledged that the courts had tended to proceed with much greater caution than happened in 1692. Belief in witchcraft was universal at the time, as much among the highly educated as the ignorant. Some people practiced forms of "white" or non-satanic magic, such as telling fortunes or casting simple spells. Far more malignant was "black" witchcraft or devil worship. It must be remembered that nothing was known of germs and little of sanitation. Satan was feared, and it was considered likely that he was doing what he could to disrupt the Godly society that had been carved out with such travail on these shores. Some sermons of Puritan clergymen may have helped to stimulate those fears. The devil would most likely tempt weak or unhappy persons with offers of unusual powers if they would serve him and disrupt their fellow townspeople. If a healthy child suddenly took sick and died, or a valued animal such as the family cow sickened and stopped giving milk, it wasn't out of the question for someone to suggest that a malignant neighbor might have put the "evil eye" on the victim. Witches were around, and certain people developed a reputation as someone not to mess with.

The business of 1692 started in Salem Village, which was still a part of Salem Town although it had been allowed to establish a separate church. While other villages such as Wenham, Manchester, Marblehead, Topsfield and Beverly had been allowed to break away from the original Salem to become towns of their own, the old town held onto municipal control over the Village. It didn't relinquish that control until 1752, when the area finally was incorporated as the town of Danvers. Salem Village in 1692 seems to have been an unhappy place. Several ministers had been called to the pastorate of the Village church, were found wanting, and were either dismissed or resigned. The newest minister, the Rev. Samuel Parris, wasn't universally admired, either. There were bitter feuds among some Village families, although these may have been overblown by later analysts and in any case did not approach Hatfield-McCoy proportions.

In the winter of 1691/2 (the Julian calendar still used by England had March 25 as the first day of the year), the young daughter and niece of Rev. Parris became subject to violent fits in which they cried out, rolled on the floor and otherwise behaved in unimaginable ways. Several other girls and women of the village eventually joined in this behavior. The village physician could find no physical explanation after examining the victims, and gave his opinion that the girls must be bewitched. Parris called in as witnesses and consultants several neighboring ministers, including the Rev. John Hale of Beverly, who later wrote: "These children were bitten and pinched by invisible agents; their arms, necks and backs turned this way and that way, and back again, so it was impossible for them to do of themselves, and beyond the power of any Epileptick Fits, or natural disease to effect." This convinced the Beverly pastor to support the witch hunt that soon followed.

After many pains were taken with them, the girls were prevailed upon to name three women as the source of their bewitchment – Tituba, Parris's West Indian slave; Sarah Good and Sarah Osborn. These were three safe targets. Sarah Good (born Sarah Soolard), originally from Wenham where she had been wrongfully deprived of her inheritance by her stepfather, was a dirty, mumbling, pipe-smoking beggar and wife of a ne'er-do-well (although, since she was the mother of a 5-year-old girl, she was hardly the elderly hag witch of legend). Sarah Osborn was a widow, ailing and friendless. She would die in prison of sickness and neglect before she could be tried, while Sarah Good eventually climbed the executioner's ladder. Tituba, whose role in stimulating the girls' imagination with voodoo tales has been greatly exaggerated, was an equally easy target. But Tituba, whether by guile or luck, discovered the one way she could save herself from hanging. As it turned out, only those who insisted on their innocence would die. Tituba was quick to confess, and vividly stimulated the authorities' imaginations by providing lurid details of how Satan was operating among them. She would be jailed and eventually sold to pay the cost of her keep, but by her "confession" she escaped the noose.

More and more "victims" of all ages soon turned up, as more and more alleged witches were cried out against. With the squalid jails overcrowded, newly appointed Royal Governor Sir William Phips moved to appoint a special Court of Oyer and Terminer to speed disposition of the cases. The surviving witch trial records are only of the preliminary examinations; all records of the special court are lost. Over the next five months the Court of Oyer and Terminer, accepting "spectral evidence" that witnesses were being tormented in court by invisible agents, condemned all of those who would hang, and a number of others who escaped with their lives one way or another. The latter would include Beverly's most infamous "witch." Eventually, such ministers as Increase and Cotton Mather grew uneasy about some of the court's methods, and certain of the judges began to have second thoughts. In October of 1692, Governor Phips dissolved the special court in favor of the regular courts, and banned spectral evidence. Slowly but surely normalcy was restored, although belief in witchcraft would continue.

Many theories have been advanced to explain the happenings of 1692. Some seem absurd, such as the suggestion that ergot mold in the grain produced hallucinations among the afflicted. Some accuse the "girls" of faking the whole thing to alleviate their boredom, although Rev. Hale's eyewitness description of the fits might call that into question. Others suggest, as Hale himself may have concluded, that they were suffering from what psychiatrists later defined as psychosomatic hysteria. It may have involved a combination, something that started for sport and got so far out of hand that the accusers came to believe that their fantasies were real. The truth may never be known. But the fascination that still prevails more than three centuries later over those tragic events of 1692 continues to attract both scholars and hordes of the merely curious.

What follows, as truthfully as we can relate it from the surviving records, is Beverly's connection to that strange time in our history. We're not looking for curious crowds or lurid sensationalism, merely to tell the truth as best we can determine from this distance in time.

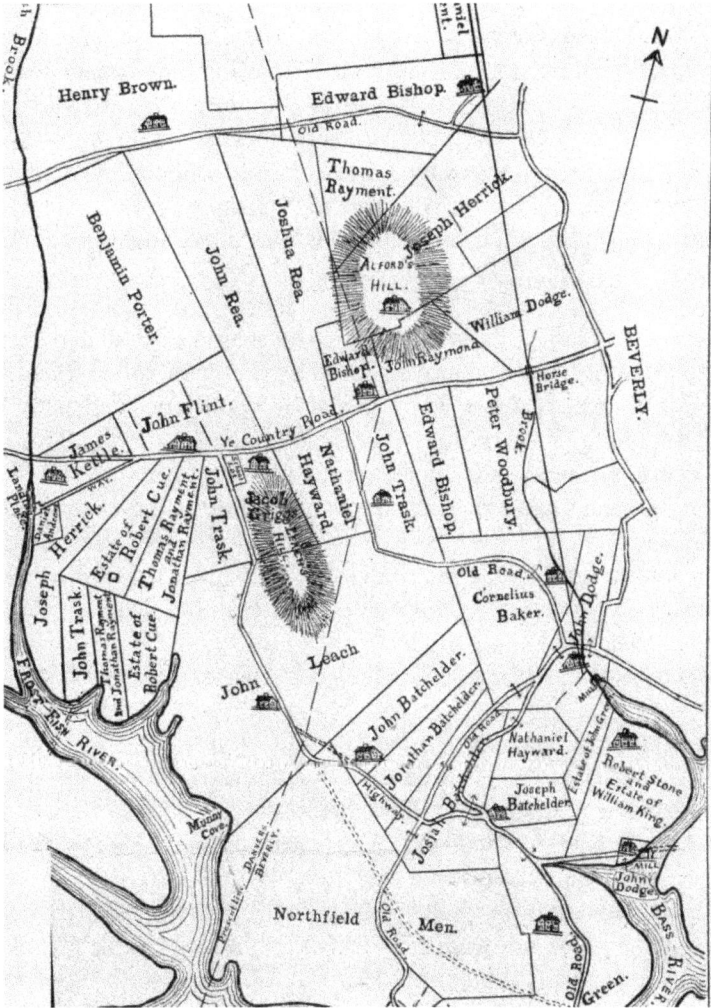

*Map from **The History of Salem Massachusetts Volume II**, by Sidney Perley*

Chapter 1: What Young David Balch Saw in His Bedroom

The John Balch House, owned by the Beverly Historical Society and Museum, is the oldest building standing in Beverly. During the summer season, it is open for tours. The oldest part is one of the most ancient structures in Massachusetts. It is not a place generally associated with the witchcraft events of 1692, but one witness's memories of a supernatural event that took place two years before the trials was an early example of the "spectral evidence" that would play such an important part in condemning innocent people to death.

John Balch, one of the five "Old Planters" who shared a 1,000 acre grant in what was to become Beverly, moved to what was then called Bass River Side and built a house here for himself and his family no later than 1638. Just how much of the present house is original has been called into question, though it is certainly not much later than the mid-17th century, but there is no disputing that John and his descendants occupied that property for many generations. John Balch died in 1648 and the house passed to his son, Benjamin. It is known that Benjamin Balch Sr. and his wife, Sarah, had 11 children. The extensive family genealogy compiled in 1898 by Galusha Balch tells us that "Benjamin Sr. lived in the old home from its building when he was nine years old, and in it all of his children were born."

Balch House had seen its share of tragedy in the early years. Benjamin Sr.'s older brother, John, was drowned while trying to cross in a boat from Salem town to Bass River. (Another brother, Freeborn, perhaps named after his father took the oath of freeman in Salem, is supposed to have abandoned Massachusetts and made the reverse migration to England.) In 1675, Joseph Balch, a son of Benjamin Sr., was 17 years old. In August of that year, despite his youth, he was allowed to enlist as a member of the "Flower of Essex," the elite company commanded by Capt. Thomas Lothrop of Beverly, part of a force of 500 soldiers being dispatched to western Massachusetts to contest the violent uprising of native Americans known as King Philip's War. While Joseph Balch's tender age makes it unlikely that he was drafted from the town militia, it can be imagined that he saw the war as a chance for adventure and begged to be allowed to go with Beverly's respected captain and town selectman. It was a fateful and fatal decision for the lad. On September 18, 1675, while Capt. Lothrop's company was guarding a train of carts carrying harvested wheat from Deerfield to military headquarters at Hadley, the men were ambushed by a force of more than 500 Indians concealed beside a stream near present South Deerfield Village that soon gained the name "Bloody Brook." Only four members of Lothrop's company survived the slaughter, in which most of the 18 Deerfield teamsters also died. All of the four Beverly men in the Flower of Essex were killed that day. Since the bodies of all of the slain were buried at Deerfield, none of the families back home, including the Balches, could have a funeral for their lost loved ones. Over the next 11 months the English settlers would take their revenge against King Philip/Metacom, chief sagamore of the Wampanoags, and his allied tribes, but that September day was a terrible blow to the towns of Essex County.

When Joseph Balch was slain, his youngest brother, David, was only four years old. It must have been difficult for the little boy to understand why his brother had marched away so proudly with his musket on his shoulder, never to return. David would live to match Joseph's age, but little beyond, as his own life would be short and difficult. It was what reportedly happened to him in the early months of 1690, when he lay bedridden at Balch House with what would prove to be a fatal illness, that later entered his name in the witch trials testimony as one of the earliest victims of spectral visitation by witches.

Bedroom of David Balch, in Beverly's Balch House.

That testimony came from Mary Gage (or Gadge), who appeared against two accused witches, Sarah Wilds and Dorcas Hoar (who has her own chapter in this account). The identity of the witness is somewhat hard to pin down. Her age is not given. Some accounts call her Gage, others Gadge; neither of those names appears in Beverly at the time. There was a Sarah Gage (or Gadge), age 40, living in Salem Village with her husband William;

they appeared as witnesses against condemned witch Sarah Good, a native of Wenham. Whether Mary was a friend of David Balch or was employed by the family as a sickroom nurse is not known, but whatever the case she had a vivid memory of being present in David's room when the young man had one of what may have been several terrifying experiences. Testifying in 1692, Mary informed the court that about two years before, she had been:

> Often concerned at the house of Benjamin Balch Sr. with his son David, being then sick. She heard said David Balch often complain that he was tormented by witches. Said deponent (meaning Mary Gage herself) "asked him whether he knew who they were. Said David Balch answered that it was Goody Wiles & her daughter & Goody Hoar & one of Marblehead he knew not by name." The young man added, according to the witness, that "there was a Confederacy of them & they were then whispering together at his bed's feet." Only David could see them. The sick youth asked another person present in the bedchamber, identified as Gabriel Hood, "to strike them & when he did strike at the place where said Balch said they sat, said Balch said he had struck Goody Wiles & she was gone presently. And at several other times said Balch cried out of Goody Hoar's tormenting him, & prayed earnestly to the Lord to bring them out & discover them & farther saith not.

In the 17th century, the appellation "Goody" was short for Goodwife. Only married women of high social standing normally were addressed as "Mrs.," while others were called goodwife or just goody. The identity of Goody Hoar could only be Beverly's infamous Dorcas, wife of William Hoar Sr. "Goody Wiles" certainly was Sarah Wilds, accused by many, who was condemned as a witch on June 30, 1692 by the Court of Oyer and Terminer and was executed in Salem on July 19, along with the conspicuously innocent Rebeckah Nurse and others. Although David Balch could not identify by name their companion, the supposed witch from Marblehead, she must have looked familiar if he knew her home town. Marblehead did at the time have its notorious "town witch," Wilmot "Mammy" Redd, also among the 20 victims of the hysteria who paid the ultimate price. Marblehead boasts of a Redd's Pond to this day, but Wilmot Redd's reputation was such that she became the subject of a children's play chant: "Old Mammy Redd/Of Marblehead/Sweet milk could turn/To mold in churn."

We know that young David Balch died on April 17, 1690, almost certainly in the same bedroom in which he had seen the witches not long before. It is easy to speculate that if he was suffering from a fever in his final illness, he might have been subject to hallucinations. That theory could be carried further to argue that his fevered mind might have conjured up images of people such as Sarah Wilds and Dorcas Hoar, who already had earned dubious reputations and might have been whispered about in the community as likely witches. But the striking aspect of the case is that it offered a chilling preview of the "spectral evidence" testimony that would so fatefully rock judges, jurors and spectators in the courtroom of 1692.

However we may want to read the case today, the fact remains that thanks to the vivid testimony of one witness, we can remember that a boy from one of Beverly's founding families was tormented by evil spirits. Beverly's famed Balch House is forever tied in with the events that led to the death of Sarah Wilds, and a close escape for Dorcas Hoar.

Chapter 2: Where John Hale Wrote His Famous Book

Hale House, sometimes referred to as Hale Farm, has been owned and maintained by the Beverly Historical Society and Museum since the Society purchased it and the large lot surrounding it for $5,000 in 1937. For the previous 80 years or so, it had been the summer home of the Bancroft family. Hale House has often been referred to as an architect's dream because it includes three distinct sections – the original 17th century house, a 1745 gambrel-roofed addition, and 19th century sections added by the Bancrofts. The oldest part was the home of the Rev. John Hale (1636-1700), first minister of Beverly. After John Hale's death it passed to his oldest son, Robert, and then to the minister's grandson, Colonel Robert Hale, who remodeled and added to the structure, changing the front door to its present location at what would become 39 Hale St. After Colonel Hale's death in 1767, family occupation ceased and the property thereafter was rented to tenant farmers. By the 1840s, ownership had passed to Hale descendant, wealthy Boston cotton merchant Thomas Poynton Bancroft and his wife, Hannah Putnam Bancroft. With the beginning of interest in the North Shore as a cooler summer alternative to the heat of the city, the Bancrofts decided to fix up their ancient house in Beverly and turn it into a summer getaway estate. Mary Carr of the Beverly Historical Society, in a paper entitled "The Hale Family House" (reprinted in the book *John Hale: A Man Beset By Witches*), points out that Thomas Poynton Bancroft repaired and remodeled the house, including removal of the huge central chimney, and also planted the beech trees that have long been a feature of the property. His son, Robert Hale Bancroft, continued the renovations, adding the 1881 and 1898 portions that represent the 19th century wing. Mary Carr wrote that it was Robert's sister, Ellen, who suggested the name "Hale Farm" in honor of their ancestral family. Robert Bancroft bequeathed the property in trust to his two daughters. After their mother, Elise Milligan Bancroft, passed away in 1936, the daughters conveyed it to the Society the following year, after an estate sale in which the furnishings were sold off. The Society was able to open it to visitors for the first time on July 13, 1938.

The oldest part of Hale House has an accepted construction date of 1694, but there are those, including researcher Allen Hovey, who have argued that is much older. The records are somewhat ambiguous. Before Beverly became a town in 1668, Salem allowed Bass River Side to construct its own meeting house in the mid-1650s, freeing the residents of that part of town from the tedious and often dangerous chore of having to cross the harbor by ferry or private boat to attend mandatory public worship in Salem. Having a meeting house did not mean they had a church, since they were still controlled by the Salem Church, but at least they could hire a preacher (teaching officer) to conduct Sabbath services. To accommodate such a person, Bass River moved in 1657 to build a "ministry house," employing Manchester carpenter John Norman to construct a house 38 feet by 17 feet, 11-foot stud, with two rooms downstairs, two upstairs and a large garret chamber "for the use of the ministry on Cape Ann Side." That plan seems much like the original part of Hale House. After two preachers came and went, the village agreed in 1664 that 28-year-old Charlestown native John Hale, son of devout blacksmith Robert Hale and a graduate of Harvard College, would take over, paying him 70 pounds a year salary and providing his firewood. Such an agreement was commensurate with what many towns paid an ordained minister; although church and state were separate, a clergyman's pay was a public obligation, and town as well as church had to agree on the hiring. John Hale and his family would occupy the ministry house. In fact, in 1670 the disgruntled previous preacher, the Rev. Jeremiah Hobart, brought a somewhat frivolous lawsuit against the Beverly selectmen and John Hale, claiming "an undue detainer of his house and lands in Beverly, which house Mr. Hale now enjoys."

After John Hale had been three years here, Bass River was allowed by Salem to organize its own church, and John Hale accepted the call to be its pastor. He could now be formally ordained; the church could adopt a covenant, enroll and dismiss members, conduct baptisms and function as an independent body within the rules of Puritan Congregationalism that prevailed in 17th century Massachusetts. With a church in place, the new town of Beverly gained complete political independence from Salem the following year. At first, the minister's house remained town property. But the record shows that in 1694, the town moved to thank John Hale for his long service and encourage his work in the ministry by granting him ownership of the house and "about two acres of land whereon he lived." Obviously the minister and his heirs gained title to considerably more land, since by the time the property passed to the Bancrofts it included both sides of the present Bancroft Avenue and ran all the way to the ocean.

John Hale would oversee the spiritual needs of his flock, both church members and non-members, who were required by law to attend public worship, for 36 years until his death. His first wife was Rebekah Byles of Salisbury; they were married the same year he came to what became Beverly. They had two children, Rebeckah (who died of tuberculosis in 1681 age 15), and Robert. After he was widowed in 1683, the minister married Sarah Noyes, youngest child of the Rev. James Noyes of Newbury, who had four children – James, Samuel (grandfather of Nathan Hale), Joanna and John. Sarah would die young in 1695. John Hale's third wife, who he married less than two years before his death, was the widow Elizabeth Clark of Newbury.

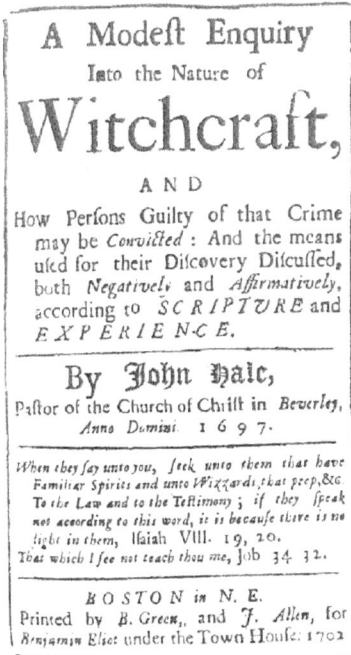

A Modeft Enquiry

Into the Nature of

Witchcraft,

AND

How Perfons Guilty of that Crime may be *Convicted* : And the means ufed for their Difcovery Difcuffed, both *Negatively* and *Affirmatively*, according to *SCRIPTURE* and *EXPERIENCE*.

By John Hale,

Paftor of the Church of Chrift in *Beverley*, Anno Domini. 1 6 9 7.

When they fay unto you, feek unto them that have Familiar Spirits and unto Wizzards that peep,&c. To the Law and to the Teftimony ; if they fpeak not according to this word, it is becaufe there is no light in them, Ifaiah VIII. 19, 20.
That which I fee not teach thou me, Job 34. 32.

BOSTON in N. E.

Printed by *B. Green,*, and *J. Allen,* for *Benjamin Elict* under the Town Houfe. 1702

Title page of John Hale's book.

But Rev. Hale's days were not always tranquil. In 1678, as related in the author's *Thieves, Cowbeaters and Other True Tales of Colonial Beverly*, the minister and his family came under assault from his vicious live-in maid, Margaret Lord, and the children of his neighbor Dorcas Hoar, who was Beverly's leading receiver of stolen goods and a woman who dabbled in things that could at the time have been considered witchcraft. A squabble between neighbors who were members of his church culminated in the violent death of a young wife and mother, which, while ruled a suicide, may not have been, as we will see in a later chapter. That incident also raised the specter of witches being about. And in 1692, John Hale found himself dragged into the events that would be remembered as "Salem Witchcraft." It has been pointed out in *John Hale: A Man Beset By Witches*, that as a boy of 12 in Charlestown, John had been a spectator at the trial and then the execution of Margaret Jones, who was condemned for witchcraft but went to her death insisting on her innocence. That must have left a lasting impression on him.

When the daughter and niece of his colleague in Salem Village, the Rev. Samuel Parris, began to behave in outlandish ways, John Hale was called into consultation. After viewing the extremity of their fits, he was convinced they could not possibly have been "faking it." That instantly made him a believer, along with others, that the devil was at work. Those fits would be the catalyst for the mass hysteria that quickly followed. John Hale would offer testimony in the trials of Sarah Bishop and Dorcas Hoar. He seems to have attended several of the trials and some of the executions. Somehow, through it all, he had to keep his own congregation instructed and comforted; he was successful in that there is no evidence of any of the sort of hysterical activity that occurred in Salem Village and Andover taking place in Beverly.

When it was all over, he had time to reflect on the errors that had taken place. Even if the 1694 date for Hale House is accurate, it was there that the Beverly minister's reflections took place. After waiting for some more learned cleric or scholar to put pen to paper, John Hale sat down in 1697 and began to write the book that would be his legacy. He called it *A Modest Enquiry Into the Nature of Witchcraft*. Completed (with a foreword by the venerable Rev. John Higginson of Salem), it would not be published until 1702, after John Hale was in his grave. "Modest" was his own choice of wording. As he himself wrote: "I have waited five years for some other person to undertake it, who might do it better than I can, but find none; and judge it better to do what I can, than that such a work should be left undone." Hale believed that his effort, "sincerely though weakly done," was preferable to nothing at all, or leaving it to someone who might "with such a bias or prejudice as will put false glosses" on the events that occurred. He took time to point that, "I have special reasons moving me to bear my testimony about these matters, before I go hence and be no more."

Hale still profoundly believed in the powers of the air, but felt it necessary to point out the need for caution to prevent a repetition of the errors that had taken place in Essex County. He painstakingly reviewed the happenings of 1692 (often using initials instead of names), as well as earlier witchcraft cases, including many Biblical references. And he felt a deep sorrow for what he now realized were gross miscarriages of justice that led to the sufferings of the innocent. In a statement that is the most profound writing in his book, one that should be memorialized at Hale Farm, John Hale declared:

> Such was the darkness of that day, the tortures and lamentations of the afflicted, and the power of former precedents that we walked in the clouds, and could not see our way. And we have most cause to be humbled for errors on that hand, which cannot be retrieved.

Author Chadwick Hansen, in *Witchcraft at Salem*, credits John Hale with an insight far ahead of his time. After quoting a passage in the *Modest Enquiry*, Hanson adds: "John Hale had discovered that the sufferings of bewitched people were psychosomatic...And recognition of that fact would make any trial for malefic witchcraft impossible. Hale's insight was brilliant. But he put it badly, and he did not insist enough upon it, so his discovery was simply lost."

John Hale's book is still available in reprints. Just as importantly, the house where he wrote it is, thanks to the Beverly Historical Society and Museum, available to visitors.

Chapter 3: How Dorcas Hoar Cheated the Hangman

If one were to try to categorize the 17th century residents of Beverly, Dorcas Hoar undoubtedly would be listed as a "town character." But although she had her colorful side, Dorcas was a town character with a malicious, if not downright malignant side. She was an accomplished thief, or perhaps it might be more accurate to call her Beverly's leading receiver of stolen goods. This writer, in conducting tours of Hale House, has sometimes half-jokingly referred to Dorcas as "the godmother of the 17th century Beverly mob." She used many associates in her quest for obtaining other people's goods, including several of her own children, and other people's servants, including perhaps the most vicious and dangerous inhabitant of the town in 1678, the Hale family's 17-year-old live-in maid, Margaret Lord. Yet even though stolen goods were found in her house, Dorcas and two of her married daughters, along with one living at home, escaped with a relatively light penalty when the case came before the court. Margaret Lord, by running away and hiding, seems to have escaped the court's wrath entirely.

The evil matriarch of the Hoar clan was born Dorcas Galley, the daughter of John Galley of Salem. She married William Hoar, a fisherman by trade, who was living on the Bass River (Beverly) Side by 1651. Their home was down the road from the ministry house. Eight children would be born to the couple, five daughters and three sons, all but two of whom were implicated in the thefts from the Rev. John Hale's parsonage that came to light in 1678. The minister and his family were far from the only victims of the widespread theft ring. Another neighbor, Josiah Rootes, told the Quarterly Court in 1678 that "for near twenty years together we have been afflicted by having our goods stolen at sundry times. And we not able to make due proof have been forced to suffer ourselves to be wronged in estate." Rootes had long suspected the Hoars, and "after my servant had acquaintance with their house, I could keep nothing in safety that lay in my servant's way." Beverly patriarch Roger Conant, who had founded Salem in 1626 before crossing to the Beverly side, told that two of William Hoar's daughters came to his door asking to buy apples. While he was going to his apple barrel, the girls disappeared, taking with them a length of his canvas. Beverly merchant Humphrey Coombs had a barrel of oil stolen, soon after which the Hoars began selling oil by the jar. A few months after the thefts were prosecuted, three of the Hoar children took their revenge on John Hale by beating the minister's cows, fatally injuring one.

Dorcas Hoar also dabbled in fortune telling. She had somehow, illicitly or otherwise, come into possession of a book on palmistry, and used it to conduct readings (presumably for a fee) and predict the future. Chadwick Hansen, in *Witchcraft at Salem*, noted that, "Fortune telling is often only white magic. But it easily becomes black magic when it concerns itself with the time or manner of the subject's death. In such cases the fortune teller is often suspected, and not without reason, of assisting fortune." Dorcas had told acquaintances that she would live poorly as long as her husband was alive, but after William's death she would live better. John Hale had discovered the fortune telling, but after counseling Dorcas that it was "an evil book and an evil art," the minister believed, wrongly, that she had agreed to give up the practice. John Hale's eldest child Rebeckah, 12 in 1678, had become aware of the thefts long before her parents did. One of the threats used to ensure her silence was that Dorcas Hoar was a witch, and, as her father later said, "had a book by which she could tell what Rebeckah did tell me in my house....." and if the thefts were mentioned "Hoar would raise the Devil to kill her or bewitch her or words to that effect." Unwilling at that time to accept such a scenario, the minister recalled that he urged his daughter "not to think so hardly of Goody Hoar." But after Rebeckah died of tuberculosis in 1681, her father learned from a friend that the girl had remained in fear of the Hoars until the end of her life.

Since Dorcas Hoar had such an evil reputation in and around Beverly, it could hardly be surprising that she would be an early target when the cry of "witchcraft" was raised early in 1692. Despite the fact that her husband, William Hoar Sr., had been elevated to the important office of sexton of the Beverly meeting house in 1680, suspicions regarding his wife's character continued to spread. As we have seen from Mary Gage's testimony, young David Balch claimed in 1690 that among the apparitions tormenting him was that of Goody Hoar. The Salem Village accusers had her on their list soon after calling down the law on their first "afflicters," Tituba, Sarah Good and Sarah Osborn. Dorcas Hoar was named in a warrant for apprehension issued on April 30, 1692 to George Herrick, marshal of Essex County. As ordered, Herrick delivered her two days later to the house where the preliminary examinations were being conducted by two Salem judges, John Hathorne and Jonathan Corwin. Several of the usual Salem Village girls were on hand. Abigail Williams claimed that Dorcas was "the first she saw before ever Tituba Indian or any other." Elizabeth Hubbard displayed a mark where she said Goody Hoar had just pinched her, and the girls claimed they could see a "black man" whispering in the accused's ear. Dorcas then angered Hathorne by crying out: "Oh! You are liars, and God will stop the mouth of liars."

Protestations of innocence did Dorcas no good, as was the case with most of those accused of witchcraft. She would be remanded to spend the hot weather months in the tender confines of a 17th century jail. While awaiting her own trial, she would learn of the hanging of Bridget Bishop in June, and the group hangings that followed in July and August. Perhaps realizing that some criticism of the proceedings was beginning to build, the Court of Oyer and Terminer accelerated its proceedings in September. The cry of "Guilty!" was heard again and again. Nine death warrants were signed for executions to be carried out on September 22. One of those was for Beverly's Dorcas Hoar. But likely after a sleepless night, early in the morning of the day before she was to be carried in a cart from the jail to the gallows, Dorcas Hoar saved herself in the only way she could. Undoubtedly remembering Tituba and others who had escaped death by uttering false confessions, Dorcas made up her mind to play her last card. Since the truth could not save her, she would tell as many lies as it might take. Undoubtedly shouting to the jailer to call in a clerk along with as many ministers and magistrates as could be quickly rounded up, Dorcas said she was ready to confess, thank you very much. Someone must have traveled in a hurry from Salem to Beverly to fetch John Hale.

The Beverly minister's own account in his book makes it apparent that Dorcas Hoar had decided to add a touch of realism to her "confession" by wounding herself, or showing the scar from an earlier injury she had received in the jail. Dorcas confessed to having signed the Devil's Book. She had furthermore afflicted a "maid" who had complained of her, "and in doing of it had received two wounds by a sword or rapier, a small one about the eye which she showed to the magistrates, and a bigger one on the side, of which she was searched by a discreet woman, who reported that D. H. had on her side the sign of a wound newly healed." Hale added: "This D. H. confessed that she was at a Witch Meeting at Salem Village, where were many persons that she named, some of whom were in Prison then or soon after upon suspicion of Witchcraft. And there the said G. B. (meaning George Burroughs, a former Salem Village pastor who was condemned as a wizard and executed) preached to them, and such a woman was their Deacon, and there they had a Sacrament." (One popular witch activity was supposed to have been a parody of the Lord's Supper.)

Dorcas Hoar's confession must have caused a sensation. A letter to Governor Phips was hastily drawn up, signed by John Hale, the Rev. Nicholas Noyes, "teacher" or associate minister of the Salem Church, and two other ministers present, urging a reprieve for Dorcas. It was dispatched to Boston by express rider, and it had the desired effect. Samuel Sewell, a judge in the witch court and future chief justice of Massachusetts, had little to say about witchcraft matters in his voluminous Diary, a treasure trove of Colonial life that has been published. But on Sept. 21, 1692, Sewell wrote this about Dorcas Hoar: "An order is sent to the sheriff to forbear her execution, notwithstanding her being in the warrant to die tomorrow. This is the first condemned person who has confessed." The next day, Sept. 22, Martha Corey, Mary Easty, Alice Parker, Ann Pudeator, Margaret Scott, Wilmot Redd, Mary Parker and Samuel Wardwell would die. But Dorcas Hoar remained in the jail. By her "confession," she had cheated the hangman.

The governor's order specified only a month's reprieve for Dorcas, but it would be enough. The September 22 executions were the last of the witchcraft hysteria. The special court would fall in October and no more weight could be given to "spectral evidence" when trials resumed by the regular courts. John Hale wrote that "Goody F.," by whom he undoubtedly meant Ann Faulkner, followed Dorcas's lead by confessing. Dorcas would remain behind bars for several months, until the jails were finally cleared in 1693. Little is known about her later life, but as a convicted and confessed witch she must have been scorned by most people. In Beverly C. Carlman's hand-written notes on file at the Beverly Historical Society and Museum, this notation appears regarding the estate of William Hoar Sr., "The widow outlawed." Contrary to her palmistry prediction, she received no legacy at all from her husband's estate, and the town records of Beverly show that in 1697 she was a pauper, supported by the town. Her keep was assigned to her son-in-law, John King Jr., who had married Dorcas's youngest daughter, Annis "Nancy" Hoar, one of the thieves of 1678 and a "cow beater" of 1679. The agreement was renewed in 1702, but there is no entry in the Vital Records of when Dorcas Hoar left this life.

Dorcas presumably died in bitterness, and probably without having sought forgiveness for her dissolute life. But that wasn't the case with one of her most ill-favored daughters, Tabitha (Tabby), who married Leonard Slew in 1678. Once a noteworthy thief in her mother's ring and a notorious liar, Tabby eventually got religion, and joined John Hale's church. The pastor recorded in the church records on December 22, 1695, that he "baptized Tabitha, wife of Leonard Slew, professing faith and repentance." Score one victory for John Hale.

Photograph from the 1890s shows former home of Dorcas Hoar on Hale Street not far from John Hale's house. It was torn down early in the 20th century.

Chapter 4: Edward and Sarah Bishop: Noisy Neighbors

The story of Edward and Sarah Bishop, who were Beverly residents despite what most accounts tell us, has become permanently conflicted and confused with that of Bridget Bishop, the first convicted witch to die by hanging on June 10, 1692. Bridget has been remembered as the keeper of a rowdy, illegal tavern in Salem Village, which she most assuredly was not. It has been reported by many authors and scholars that Bridget was a parishioner of the Rev. John Hale, and that the Beverly pastor testified against her. Neither statement is true. She has been accused of being an outrageous liar because she testified in court that she had never been to Salem Village. Whatever faults Bridget Bishop may have had, and her reputation preceded the witchcraft allegations, it is highly unlikely that she perjured herself on that occasion. She lived in Salem Town, not the Village, and possibly never had occasion to visit the outlying district. She never lived in Beverly. Two maps of 17th century Beverly, both drawn up in the 19th century, do show the house of Bridget Bishop, and one even has the notation "hanged for a witch." But it should be safe to conclude that the historians who drew those maps were under the long-held mistaken impression that Reverend Hale had testified against Bridget.

When the original hand-written records of the witchcraft proceedings were transcribed in 1937 as a Depression-era Works Progress Administration project, the old heading "John Hale Against Bridget Bishop" was retained, and so it appears in the printed version available to researchers since that time. As a result, Bridget (Oliver) Bishop has taken on the false image of a wanton woman who kept a tavern. As Bernard Rosenthal tells us in his 1993 *Salem Story*, "Bridget Bishop has appeared as something of a folk heroine in Salem's story; a spirited, feisty, perhaps lusty woman – an American Wife of Bath, sometimes – who flaunted Puritan mores with a happy public house where drinking and gambling, and insinuated wenching, occurred." None of it is true, of course, as Rosenthal points out. Beverly researcher Marguerite Harris, co-author of *John Hale: A Man Beset By Witches* at first accepted the traditional account, but later discovered the cause for the error and inserted a corrected explanation. Hidden in a crease of the original manuscript, overlooked for years, is the inscription, "John Hale agn'st Sarah Bishop." Although Hale seems to have attended Bridget Bishop's execution, he never testified against her. Further muddying the waters is the fact that Bridget's husband also was named Edward Bishop. Numerous authors and researchers have been misled. John Hale appeared against his own parishioner, Sarah (Wilds) Bishop, husband of Edward Bishop (also accused of witchcraft). At the time of the trials, Edward Bishop, born in Salem in 1648, was 44 years old; Sarah, who may have been a native of Topsfield, was 41.

In most accounts, Edward and Sarah Bishop are said to be residents of Salem Village. But a detailed map of the period, in the possession of the Beverly Historical Society and Museum, puts their house and property on what is now the Beverly-Danvers line, the present Conant Street. That explains why they were members of the Beverly church, not the one in the Village. When the original "Country Road" was established in the 1640s as a public highway, it passed south through Newbury, Rowley, Ipswich and Wenham, roughly following the path of present Route 1A. After crossing into Beverly, it turned west along Conant Street into Salem Village (Danvers, from where a side road led to Salem Town), then headed south toward Boston through what is now Peabody, Saugus (then part of Lynn) and Rumney Marsh (Chelsea). As the main highway south to north, it was heavily traveled. If Edward and Sarah Bishop had wanted to run a tavern, their homestead on an isolated part of the main highway might seem an ideal spot. But just doing so on their own wouldn't be an easy undertaking. To operate an "ordinary," or "house of publick entertainment" required a license from the town, and the sale of alcoholic beverages was tightly controlled by the Great and General Court. A bootleg operation would soon come to the attention of and be disputed by the licensed innkeepers of the area. Not that Edward Bishop hadn't tried to sell illicit booze, and on one occasion he was fined for it, according to Rosenthal. Perhaps he and Sarah just liked to attract company to their home after hours, to play "shovelboard" and other noisy sports which the authorities frowned upon. If somebody wanted to wet their throat with a glass of beer or hard cider, why not?

John Hale's testimony, for so long wrongfully pointed at Bridget Bishop, revolved around an account of a dispute between Sarah and her neighbor, Christian Trask, which will be examined in much more detail in the next chapter. Christian Trask complained to the Beverly minister about the disturbances taking place at the home of her neighbors, the Bishops, and that she had received no satisfaction when she confronted Sarah about it. Rosenthal takes note that two of the frequent witch accusers, Sarah Churchill and Susannah Sheldon, hearing second hand about John Hale's testimony against "Goodwife Bishop," thought it meant Bridget and further confused things by making up a story involving Bridget.

While most of the testimony regarding the Bishops can't be retrieved, we do have a deposition of Elizabeth Balch, another member by marriage of Beverly's Balch House family. Benjamin Balch Jr., a son of Benjamin Sr. and Sarah (Gardner) Balch, a grandson of Old Planter John, brother of Joseph and "bewitched" David, was born in 1653. Infant baptism was standard at the time, but his father, liberal in religious matters, decided to allow his children the choice of whether and when to be baptized. Young Benjamin, according to the Balch Genealogy, was baptized at his own desire as a teenager on April 10, 1670. On October 11, 1674, he was married to Elizabeth Woodbury, daughter of John and Elizabeth. They would have six children, and Benjamin received 25 acres of land in Beverly from his father.

Elizabeth Balch gave a deposition to the court which makes clear that Edward and Sarah Bishop not only were an argumentative couple, but that he had no compunction about calling his own wife a witch. Elizabeth did not give a specific date to the incident, but said it happened on the "very day that Captain George Corwin was buried." Goodwife Balch recalled that she was returning home from Salem to Beverly via the Village in the evening, riding double on horseback with her then unmarried sister Abigail Woodbury, soon to be the wife of Nathaniel Waldron of Wenham. As they approached what was known as Crane River Common, they were overtaken by Edward Bishop and his wife, also on horseback, "who are both now in prison under suspicion of witchcraft." At the time, the Bishops "had some words of difference, it seemed unto us." Edward Bishop, holding the reins, guided the horse into a brook, wetting his wife. Sarah, livid, found "fault with his so doing, and said he would throw her into the water or words to that purpose." Her husband's reply, according to Elizabeth Balch, was that "it was no matter if he did." While the four continued to ride together toward Beverly, the Bishops resumed their quarrel. Sarah scolded Edward for riding too fast, and said she thought he "would do her a mischief." Her loving husband replied "that it was no matter what was done unto her, or words to that effect." Then addressing his speech to Elizabeth and Abigail, he told them that Sarah "had been a bad wife to him ever since they were married." Lately, she had been worse than ever. Not only that, said he, "the Devil had come bodily unto her....." and that she had "sat up all the night long with the Devil." He kept up his accusations of his wife as a witch "until we came to said Bishops' dwelling house." Elizabeth said Sarah had little to say during the tirade. Before they parted, Goodwife Balch said she "reproved" Edward Bishop for speaking in such a way about his spouse, but his only reply was that it was "nothing but what was truth." Elizabeth Balch signed her statement with a mark, and Abigail Waldron added her mark in witness.

After their April arrest, the Bishops were put in jail, but never were tried for witchcraft. In fact, the couple allegedly escaped from prison and went into hiding before any trial could take place. One story is that they fled to the New York colony, and remained there until 1693, when they felt it was safe to return home. After their escape, Sheriff George Corwin (a nephew of the judge) seized their property, which would have been illegal. Bernard Rosenthal speculates that the sheriff contrived, or even faked, the escape in an attempt to justify the seizure. In any event, citing as his source Robert Calef's *More Wonders of the Invisible World*, Rosenthal wrote that Samuel Bishop, a son of the couple, had to fork over 10 pounds to redeem his parents' property. Whatever the case, the Bishops survived their ordeal and returned home. In the Beverly Vital Records (Vol. 1, p. 44) is listed the baptism on May 12, 1695 of Ebenezer Bishop, son of Edward and Sarah. That might have been pushing things, since Sarah was 44 by that year, but Ebenezer could have been born earlier and his baptism put off until after all of the witchcraft business had calmed down. According to one genealogical record, Edward and Sarah at some point moved to Rehoboth in Bristol County, where he died on May 12, 1711 and she soon thereafter. Wherever the couple spent their final years, presumably there was no more domestic talk of witchcraft.

Beverly's Abbot Street burial grounds c. 1915, where the tombstones of the Rev. John Hale and some of his family members can be found.

Chapter 5: Was Christian Trask Murdered?

In the previous chapter, we met accused witches Edward and Sarah Bishop, whose story has been conflicted and confused with that of Bridget (Oliver) Bishop, the first to be convicted and hanged in Salem. In that account there was a brief reference to their neighbor, Christian Trask, dead almost three years before the witch trials, but whose short, unfortunate life ties in with the tale of the Bishops.

Christian Trask was born Christian Woodbury on April 20, 1661, when Beverly was still the Bass River Side section of Salem. Her parents were Humphrey Woodbury Sr., one of the early settlers of Bass River and a founder of Beverly, and his wife, Elizabeth. When Humphrey Woodbury's will was probated in 1686, it mentioned his widow and nine children: sons Richard, Thomas, John, Isaac, William and Humphrey Jr.; married daughters Susannah Teny, Christian Trask and Elizabeth Walker. On April 9, 1679 in Beverly, Christian was married to John Trask. He was the son of Osmond and Elizabeth Trask, who also were early Beverlyites. The births of five children to the couple were recorded between 1680 and 1689, all of whom were baptized by the Rev. John Hale, sure evidence that the Trasks were members of the Beverly Church. The oldest child, a daughter named Christian after her mother, died in 1687 at age seven. Surviving children were John, Edward, Elizabeth and William, born at the beginning of 1689.

Beverly C. Carlman, in her research of early Beverly families, noted that John Trask, who died in 1720 at about 62, had lived on what is now Grover Street in the Centerville section of Beverly. In 1715, five years before he died, John sold to Robert Morgan, cooper, "my mansion house with the barn, outbuildings (and) 20 acres." But since evidence points to the Trasks and Bishops as being neighbors in the 1680s, when the Bishops resided on what is now Conant Street, the Trasks must then have lived near Edward and Sarah. In fact, the same map that shows the Bishop lot straddling the present Beverly-Danvers line places the Trask homestead just to the south, on a lane running from Ye (the) Country Road (Conant Street). That would have placed it in the domain of Ryal Side, still part of Salem Town although geographically tied to Beverly. Since 1692 was 20 years before establishment of the Second Parish at North Beverly, the area came under the domain of John Hale's church.

Young Goodwife Trask seems to have suffered from mental illness that became a grave concern to John Hale, who did what he could to help her. It is also evident from Hale's own testimony that he believed she could have been a victim of witchcraft three years before the events of Salem Village. Christian Trask had learned to read and write, a remarkable accomplishment in an era when girls normally didn't go to school and many men signed their names with a mark. She seems to have quarreled with the Bishops on more than one occasion, apparently over the latter couple's keeping rowdy company at late hours and playing "shovel board," the game played with wooden pieces now better known as shuffleboard. One evening Christian Trask, whether under one of her fits or just angry at the disturbance that might have been keeping her young children awake, entered the Bishops' place, seized the wooden implements of the game, and threw them into the fireplace. Rev. Hale later testified that Christian "had reproved the said Bishop for promoting such disorders, but received no satisfaction from her about it."

In his 1692 court testimony in the case of Sarah Bishop, John Hale recorded that "about 5 or 6 years ago," meaning in 1686 or 1687, the quarrel between the neighbors became heated. He recalled that "Christian the wife of John Trask (living in Salem bounds bordering of the above said Beverly), being in full communion in our Church, came to me to request that Goodwife Bishop her Neighbor, wife of Edward Bishop Jr., might not be permitted to receive the Lord's Supper in our church till she had given ...satisfaction from her offenses...because the said Bishop did entertain people in her house at unseasonable hours of the night to keep drinking and playing at shovel-board, whereby discord did arise in other families, and young people were in danger to be corrupted..." It was about that time that Christian staged her raid and destroyed the game pieces.

The Beverly minister tried to bring peace between the members of his church, especially as Christian Trask's emotional "distractions" worsened over time. But early in 1689, she seemed to grow better. John Hale reported on what might have been his last meeting with Christian:

> I was praying with and counseling of Goody Trask before her death, and not many days before her end, being there, she seemed more rational and earnestly desired Edward Bishop might be sent for that she might make friends with him. I asked her if she had wronged Edward Bishop. She said not that she knew of, unless it were in taking his shovel-board pieces when people were at play with them and throwing them into the fire. If she did evil in it she was very sorry for it and desired that he would be friends with her or forgive her. This was the very day before she died, or a few days before.

The pastor did not record whether the desired meeting took place. But he did note that "the Sabbath before she died, I received a note for prayers on her behalf, which her husband said was written by herself, and I judge was her own handwriting, being well acquainted with her hand." That written statement of testimony was signed by John Hale on May 20, 1692. He informed the court that "several parts of this testimony" could be confirmed by "Major Gedney, Mr. (Samuel) Parris, Joseph Herrick Jr. and his wife, John Trask, Margaret King, Hannah wife of Colonel Baker" and others.

His description of the written note is proof of Christian Trask's literacy, and one can hope that John Hale did indeed step before the Beverly congregation and offer special prayers for the young wife and mother.

But on June 23, 1689, Christian Trask was found dead, her throat cut and a small pair of scissors lying nearby. Whether it happened in her house or elsewhere is not mentioned, but it must have been an especially bloody ending. John Hale was called to view the body. The minister was not a medical doctor, unlike John Fiske, first pastor of the Wenham church, who combined medicine with preaching. But Hale was a well educated man, and obviously had considerable knowledge of anatomy. While we are trying to avoid sensationalism, it is important to include his description of the 28-year-old wife's fatal wounds, since they pose a major question.

> As to the wounds she died of, I observed 3 deadly ones. A piece of her windpipe cut out, and another wound below that, through the windpipe and gullet to the vein they call jugular. So that I then judged and still do apprehend it impossible for her with so short a pair of scissors to mangle herself so, without some extraordinary work of the devil or witchcraft.

Hale speaks of three "deadly wounds" but he only describes two, meaning that a third deep cut must have appeared in Christian Trask's throat.

As with any unexplained or violent death, a jury of inquest was convened by the county court the next day, June 24. Its members included Joshua Rea Jr., James Putnam, Edward Bishop Jr. (Christian's neighbor and adversary), Joseph Herrick, Daniel Andrew, Nathaniel Hayward, Thomas Rayment, Benjamin Balch, James Kettle and William Rayment Jr. The conclusion of the jury was that Christian Trask had taken her own life, and the report was entered into the court record.

But how could she have? The jurors, of course had no knowledge of forensics and no autopsy was ordered. All they had to go on was a young woman dead of a mangled throat, and a pair of scissors – short scissors – beside the body. Blood samples, fingerprints or pathology tests lay far in the future. There were no witnesses. The obvious conclusion for a 17th century jury of inquest made up of inexperienced citizens (such violent deaths being rare occurrences) was that she had killed herself, and at least one member of the jury must have been eager to support that ruling. But any modern crime scene investigator or criminal pathologist would say it was impossible for any person to take their own life by inflicting multiple fatal wounds to the throat. How could a woman cut a piece out of her own gullet with a pair of probably dull scissors, inflict a second slash, then have the strength and will to follow up by stabbing right through the windpipe to the jugular? John Hale himself was incredulous at the conclusion of suicide, unless, as he said, the victim had been under the influence of "the devil or witchcraft." Mental illness was very poorly understood, but nobody had accused poor Christian Trask of being in league with the devil. Even if she was suffering from depression, she had four young children to care for, including an infant.

The obvious conclusion, which can't be "proved" except through application of common sense, is that she was the victim of a brutal murder, with the killer leaving the short scissors beside the body to make it look like suicide. Who could have done it? An obvious suspect would be Edward Bishop, who had long feuded with his neighbor. Her attempts at "making friends" with him could have provoked a long-simmering resentment over the shovel-board incident. Someone might also point a finger at John Trask. Maybe he could have become so discouraged by his wife's distractions that he thought he might be better off with her out of the way. But to think that a man who seems to have had a good reputation, and who lived as a respected member of the community for 30 years after the event, could have conceived of and carried out such a bloody, brutal deed, is beyond belief. Left with four small children to raise alone, John Trask remarried on Oct. 20, 1690, taking for his second wife Mary Dodge of Salem. They had one child, and after Mary's death John Trask's third wife, Elizabeth, presented him with three more children. The youngest, born in 1701, was a daughter who would be given the name Christian.

The bloody death of Goodwife Trask remains a mystery. But it also remains tainted on the record with the specter of witchcraft.

Chapter 6: The Minister's Wife as a "Specter"

A few years ago, while this writer was working a volunteer shift at the Beverly Historical Society's Cabot House Museum, a call came in from a researcher who had a question: Why, he demanded, did the Beverly Historical Society take the official position that the incident involving John Hale's wife had "put an end" to the Salem witchcraft prosecutions? After being assured that the Society did not have such an official position, he replied by reading from an article published sometime in the past in which a B.H.S. representative was credited with telling the story roughly as follows:

1. In 1692, the wife of the Rev. John Hale of Beverly was accused of being a witch. (That was Sarah Noyes Hale, the minister's second spouse.)

2. Her friends and neighbors, knowing of her unblemished character, were scandalized and infuriated that such a ridiculous charge could be made.

3. Her husband, who had ardently supported the witch hunt, now realized it had all been a terrible mistake, and became a foe of the proceedings.

4. The resulting uproar put an end to the witch trials and restored sanity to Essex County.

It's a nice story, and while it contains a bit of truth, it does not, like many nice stories, stand up well to factual analysis. It has been told so many times that, like the myth of Abner Doubleday's "invention" of baseball, it has come to be widely accepted. Our caller was assured that while we like to think the Hale incident played a part, we are well aware that it didn't "end the witchcraft."

Yet it would be very unfair to point a finger of criticism at Beverly Historical Society and Museum members, as well as other residents of Beverly, who have confidently repeated the tale over the past century, at least. The story has been told to and by official state sources. In fact, a commemorative historical marker that has stood by the sidewalk outside Hale House for more than eight decades repeats the traditional interpretation. It is one of the few remaining signs erected in 1930 by the Massachusetts Bay Colony Historical Commission to mark the 300th anniversary of the arrival of John Winthrop with the original Massachusetts charter. It designates Hale Farm as the home of the Rev. John Hale, and then adds these words: "A charge of witchcraft against his wife convinced the minister of the folly and wickedness of the crusade and ended all witch-hunting in Beverly." So there it is, a state agency's approved statement erected for residents and tourists to quote from over the ensuing years. At least it just reads "in Beverly," not Salem or anywhere else.

So what are the facts, as best we can piece them together after more than three centuries?

The incident survives in only one document in the Massachusetts Archives, a document that leaves some questions unanswered. On November 14, 1692, a meeting took place involving the Rev. John Hale of Beverly, the Rev. Joseph Gerrish of Wenham, and a 17-year-old girl named Mary Herrick, who had a strange tale to tell the two ministers. The place of the meeting is not specified, although tradition puts it in the Wenham Historical Association's Claflin-Richards House, where Mr. Gerrish and his family were then living. Joseph Gerrish, a native of Newbury, had come to Wenham early in 1674 to replace the Rev. Antipas Newman. Mr. Newman, husband of Elizabeth Winthrop, granddaughter of the founding governor of the Massachusetts Bay Colony, died in October 1672 during Wenham's "spotted fever" (probably scarlet fever) epidemic. Antipas Newman had helped to ordain John Hale in 1667, and Beverly's church stepped in to help in Wenham's time of difficulty. During the time between Newman's death and the arrival of Gerrish, John Hale baptized the children of several Wenham church members. Rev. Gerrish, who was Wenham's pastor for 45 years, was a close friend from boyhood in Newbury of Samuel Sewell, one of the witchcraft court judges. But unlike John Hale, there is no evidence that the Wenham minister played any role in the witch trials. The identity of Mary Herrick remains a mystery. The Vital Records of the neighboring towns do not reveal anyone of that name who would have been 17 at the time. The closest found so far is a daughter of Ephraim and Mary (Crosse) Herrick, born in Beverly June 14, 1667, which would have made her 25 if still unmarried in 1692.

Mary Herrick, whoever she was, told a tale that must have transfixed the two ministers. She had been visited, she insisted (Chadwick Hansen, *Witchcraft at Salem*, p. 259) by apparitions, notably those of Mary Easty (one of the last hanged on September 22), and the wife of John Hale. The latter was said to have asked Herrick if she thought she was a witch, but the girl said she answered, "No, you be the Devil," meaning Satan appearing in Mrs. Hale's shape. Mary Easty's ghost said her mission was to vindicate her cause, proclaim her innocence and seek vengeance. If Mary Herrick told her story to the two ministers, she was assured that neither she nor Mrs. Hale would trouble her in the future.

Just how far and wide the story traveled at the time is unknown. Neither John Hale nor Joseph Gerrish was the type to spread scandal, especially if it involved someone dear or close to them. Mary Herrick was surely happy to be rid of her apparitions. Obviously, the story was dictated to some clerk or official person, since the written record survives. But it could have had little impact on the overall witchcraft picture. For one thing, the Court of Oyer and Terminer had fallen in October, with Governor Phips assigning disposition of the remaining cases to the Court of Judicature. It is also important to realize that "spectral evidence" was no longer to be given any weight in determining guilt, so a tale such as Mary Herrick's would not have been admissible as evidence against any accused person. By the fall of 1692 some of the accusers had overreached, bringing charges against prominent persons who had the wherewithal to fight back. There is no record that any complaint of witchcraft ever was lodged against Sarah Noyes Hale, and it is safe to say she was in no danger of being dragged off to prison – something her husband would have fought tooth and nail to prevent. There would continue to be trials of previously indicted persons after October, but all but a small number ended in not guilty verdicts and the few persons convicted had no fear of being executed. Certainly the incident must have shaken John Hale, but only temporarily. Nowhere in his *Modest Enquiry* did he make any reference to the story involving his wife, who had passed from this world two years before he wrote his book. But, John Hale warned in his Chapter X: "Another unsafe principle is to lay weight upon the testimony of Ghosts, as they are called; that is to say, Spectres appearing in the shape of the dead, and personating them."

We certainly should tell the story of Sarah Noyes Hale. It is part of Beverly's connection, and the Hale House connection, to the events of 1692. But we must avoid imputing more importance to it than the facts call for, despite long-standing traditions and commemorative markers.

Chapter 7: Devil's Boss and 'Mass Killer' Job Tookey, Plus Others

In addition to those already written of, a few other residents of Beverly also crop up in the witchcraft records of 1692. One of those is Job Tookey, of whom we know very little other than that he was living in Beverly at the time. His point of origin is obscure. The only Job Tookey whose birth appears in the Mormon Family Search website was born in England on March 10, 1650 and baptized at St. Albans, Hertfordshire, on May 26 of that year. His father's name is also listed as Job Tookey, no further information. If that was indeed Beverly's Job, he would have been 42 at the time of the witchcraft delusion. He is listed in one place as a "laborer," in another as a "sailor," with Beverly as his home.

How Tookey ever came to the attention of those who were calling out supposed witches and wizards is unknown. He was charged with having uttered the statement that "he was not the Devil's servant, but the Devil was his." It was the sort of half-joking comment that might be expected from an unlearned person. Tookey also is supposed to have said he would "take Mr. Burroughs' part." George Burroughs, a former pastor of the ill-favored Salem Village Church, had moved to southern Maine, then part of Massachusetts. Some of the "afflicted girls" claimed to have seen a minister appear among the witches. It was then remembered that George Burroughs had boasted of his physical strength, and had proved it with such feats as lifting a wooden barrel by the bung hole. Obviously, such power was beyond the ability of an ordinary man, and must therefore have been gained by diabolical means. Burroughs was arrested, dragged back to Salem, tried for witchcraft, convicted and executed. How Job Tookey knew him was not explained.

For whatever their motive, some of the accusers decided to take aim at Tookey not so much as a witch but rather as a mass murderer. At his preliminary examination, Salem Village girls Susannah Sheldon, Mary Warren (first an accuser, later one of those accused after she reneged), Ann Putnam and Elizabeth Booth gave magistrates John Hathorne, Jonathan Corwin and Bartholomew Gedney an earful. They claimed to see the specters of three women, three men and two children, all in winding sheets looking "red upon Tookey" and calling for vengeance. The deaths over the past two years of everyone at Ryal Side (then still part of Salem although tied to Beverly), were blamed on Job Tookey. The defendant offered the explanation, which others including Rebecca Nurse had tried without success, that "it is the Devil afflicting people in his shape, rather than him." Not surprisingly, the magistrates, eager to believe the most outrageous testimony, ordered Tookey to prison.

He turned out to be one of the lucky ones. For some reason, his trial for witchcraft did not take place until January of 1693, long after the special court had been terminated and such antics as were displayed at the preliminary hearing were no longer allowed. Even though that session of the court was headed by Lieutenant Governor William Stoughton, who had perhaps been the most rabid of the earlier judges, hard evidence was lacking. On Jan. 11, not guilty verdicts were returned for Margaret Jacobs, Sarah Buckley, Mary Witheridge, Johanna Taylor, Job Tookey and a slave named Candy. Before another four months had passed, Governor Phips ordered the withdrawal of any remaining complaints pertaining to witchcraft, and all of the jails had been cleared of the suffering innocent.

We don't know whether Job Tookey and the others were forced to spend up to seven months in the squalid jails, but it seems likely. Releasing any accused witch on bail would have been considered unthinkable. Even though lengthy travel was then not allowed except on official business, and poor strangers were unwelcome anywhere, it is certain that any person accused of a capital crime who had relatives or friends outside the area would have taken the opportunity to flee. Since Salem and Beverly were port towns, places could be sought on outgoing vessels either as paying passengers or crew. The latter choice would have been ideal for Tookey. But even though the feeling of freedom must have been a great relief in January, such a long time spent in unspeakably wretched conditions and without proper diet must have taken a heavy toll on the health of the prisoners. They also would have a hard time trying to resume normal lives. Job Tookey seems not to have remained in Beverly after his release, and who could blame him?

In addition to Tookey, a couple of other Beverly names are mentioned as possible witches. On the same day (April 30, 1692) that the magistrates drew up the order to George Herrick to arrest Dorcas Hoar, they also directed the marshal to bring in another Beverly woman, identified as Sarah Murrill. Marshal Herrick, as ordered, said he delivered the two women on May 2, 1692 to the Salem Village "ordinary" (tavern) of Lt. Nathaniel Ingersall, which they had chosen as the site for their preliminary examinations of the accused. While "spectral evidence" went on display against Dorcas Hoar that day, causing Hathorne and Corwin to come down hard on her, there is no further reference to her co-defendant. Perhaps the "afflicted girls" decided they had made a mistake in identity, or they had no more evidence to present. But any thought that Sarah might have been released is negated in the hand-written notes of Beverly C. Carlman on file at the Beverly Historical Society and Museum. Mrs. Carlman found evidence that Sarah Murrill was sent to jail in May of 1692 and remained there until January, the same month in which Job Tookey and his fellow defendants finally were released. Sarah is identified as the daughter of Peter Murrill (also called Peter Morey). In the court roster of Beverly residents who took the "Oath of Fidelity" on Jan. 3, 1677, Peter Murrill is one of 35 men who gave their occupation as fisherman, showing how popular that occupation was in the 17th century. Another Beverly woman who came under suspicion was elderly widow Susannah Rootes, but she was fortunate enough to escape any trial. Susannah was the widow of Josiah Rootes, one of the victims of the 1678 theft ring, who died in 1683. She was said to be "about 67" in 1692, but that may have been conservative. According to the Quarterly Court Records (Volume 9), Susannah petitioned the court in June of 1683 to be released as executor of her husband's estate, citing her "many weaknesses and infirmities of old age." On May 3, 1684, the court ordered that Ambrose Gale be awarded the remainder of what Josiah Rootes had left to his widow, given that Gale had maintained the widow for several months at his own expense, as long as he agreed to continue to do so for her remaining years. On May 9, 1687 (Carlman papers), Jonathan Rootes of Beverly sold land to Nehemiah Grover, two acres of which was to be devoted to "my mother Susannah Rootes for her comfortable maintenance."

The "evidence" against Susannah Rootes in 1692 was so third-hand as to be laughable. Carol F. Karlsen in her book *The Devil in the Shape of a Woman*, citing as her source the "The Salem Witchcraft Papers," edited by Boyer and Nussenbaum, writes that one Andrew Elliott appeared before the judges to inform them he had heard an unidentified man who once "lived with" (apparently meaning boarded with) Susannah Rootes, say that she was a "bad woman." Her greatest sin was to have absented herself on occasion from family prayer. Perhaps a roast being prepared for dinner called for her attention at the time others in the household were praying, but during the witchcraft delusion any instance of neglecting Christian duty might be viewed as evidence that Satan had the upper hand on a person.

Considering how many "witches" were accused, Beverly escaped without too much damage. Still, we can visit a couple of well-preserved places associated with some of the colony's most unhappy history – the doleful episode of 1692.

Here Lyes ye body of ye
Reverend Mr. John Hale
A pious & faithfull Minister
Of ye Gospel & Pastor of ye
First gathered Church of
Christ in this town of
Beverly, who rested from his
Labors on ye 15th day of May
Anno Domini 1700
In ye 64th year of his age

Text from tombstone of Reverend John Hale

For Further Reading

For those interested in reading more about the Salem witch trials and the era in which they took place, may we suggest:

Boyer, Paul and Nussenbaum, Stephen, *Salem Possessed*, Cambridge, Mass., Harvard University Press, 1974

Brown, Edward R., *Thieves, Cowbeaters and Other True Tales of Colonial Beverly,* Beverly Historical Society and Museum, 2007

Hansen, Chadwick, *Witchcraft At Salem*, New York, New American Library, 1969

Harris, Marguerite, et. al., *John Hale: A Man Beset By Witches*, Beverly Historical Society and Museum, 1992 (includes a reprint of John Hale's 'A Modest Enquiry Into the Nature of Witchcraft')

Rosenthal, Bernard, *Salem Story: Reading the Witch Trials of 1692*, Cambridge University Press, 1993

Starkey, Marion L., *The Devil in Massachusetts,* New York, Alfred A. Knopf, 1950

Trask, Richard B., *'The Devil Hath Been Raised,'* Danvers, Mass. Historical Society, by Phoenix Publishing, West Kennebunk, Maine, 1992

www.ingramcontent.com/pod-product-compliance
Lightning Source LLC
Chambersburg PA
CBHW031335040426
42443CB00005B/362